HOW TO
BECOME
A
MEDICAL
INTERPRETER

MANDARIN
繁體中文

MEGAN TSANG

How to Become a Medical Interpreter – Mandarin
Traditional Chinese Edition

STOREHOUSE PUBLISHING COMPANY
539 W. Commerce St #2278
Dallas, TX 75208
info@storehousepub.com

E-book ISBN: 978-1-7357927-0-5
Paperback ISBN: 978-1-7357927-2-9

Disclaimer:
The content of this book is for informational purposes only. The publisher and the author disclaim all such representations and warranties for a particular purpose or result. In addition, the publisher and the author assume no responsibility for errors, inaccuracies, omissions, or any other inconsistencies herein.

Printed in the United States of America

DEDICATION

I want to attribute this book to all who have made a positive impact in my life. And to my dearest Mom, Dad, the world's best brothers, my blessed sons, and my best friend: Thank you for always being there for me. This book is for you.

TABLE OF CONTENTS

BASIC ANATOMY DIAGRAMS

CHAPTER 1

INTRODUCTION

I was a career changer, just like some of you. After many years of finding my way through a process, I am now a CHI-certified medical interpreter.

This book aims to present a roadmap for anyone who is getting ready for a fulfilling career in medical interpreting. Maybe you are a career-changer looking for advice on how to become a medical interpreter. Perhaps you have just been offered a job as a medical interpreter and you want to brush up on medical terminologies. Or you may have been in this field for a few years and are wondering to yourself if there is room to grow.

You will find this book is a great resource for both new and seasoned interpreters. Rather than a lengthy glossary of anatomy, you can reference the anatomy using anatomical diagrams at the end of the book. I encourage you to look up and label the anatomical parts in your primary language, because it is an excellent way to learn them. Having a way to visualize descriptive statements are very helpful when interpreting complicated medical conditions.

The medical terminology chapters are organized from the perspective of an interpreter. It involves organizing the medical glossary in the same order for a patient's visit from the beginning to the end. No more flipping the pages back and forth, because these chapters follow you along with each session beautifully. I think you are going to love it. Happy interpreting.

CHAPTER 2

QUALIFICATION

Just like being able to do arithmetic does not qualify someone to be an accountant; fluency in a language does not qualify someone to be an interpreter. The number one myth about the role of medical interpreter is that anyone who is bilingual is capable of interpreting. Well, that is not entirely true because interpreting is so much more than helping two parties communicate. Competent interpreters must strive to render the meaning of what someone says accurately without omission or addition. Integrity and impartiality are the top reasons for using a qualified professional interpreter to foster communication. And it is even more true in the healthcare settings.

Hiring companies look for near-native levels of ability in two languages. One is called the target language, and another one is the source language. In other words, hiring companies are looking for candidates who can proficiently converse back and forth from the source to the target language and vice versa. Therefore, if you are more comfortable with interpreting from Chinese to English, then you will need to practice more on interpreting from English to Chinese.

An interpreter needs to be quick to listen and be ready to render what was said. An interpreter remembers what he or she hears by utilizing notetaking and memory-recall techniques. Here, the goal of notetaking is to write just enough information so the interpreter can recall, reconstruct, and deliver it in the target language. I use abbreviations, symbols, and drawings in my notetaking. Lastly, it is also essential for interpreters to maintain their composure in stressful situations. But do not be dismayed at the long list of skill sets needed, because you probably have acquired these skills from your education and work experiences.

When you look at the job descriptions listed by the hiring companies, you will notice that the required education and experience levels vary slightly from one company to the next. For example, one company might consider candidates with one to two years of interpreting experience. Another company could require a national level certification with skills specifically in healthcare interpreting. For a new jobseeker, your goal is to get your foot in the door. You may have to be willing to work earlier than usual or to take a graveyard shift. You may also have to work as a translator as a stepping-stone.

Regardless, all hiring companies will ask you to take an oral test over the phone as part of the job-application process. There are thousands of medical terminologies out there. However, you do not need to wait until you have memorized them all to begin the job search. One way to quickly prepare for the oral test is by studying the vocabulary provided in this book. The medical terminologies included in this guide are high-frequency vocabularies that you will most often encounter on the job. They are a great way to jumpstart your word bank. Whether you make them into index cards or write them on sticky notes and decorate your walls with them, repetitions of these terms will commit them to your long-term memory. I included mock-up scenarios to help you practice.

CHAPTER 3

JUMPING OVER HURDLES

The biggest hurdle to entering this field is a lack of experience. You might ask where someone can get interpretation experience. There are many places where you may find opportunities to work as a volunteering interpreter, such as free clinics, non-profit organizations, religious organizations, and schools. I remember seeing bilingual moms helping Spanish-speaking families register their children in my neighborhood's elementary school. Also, many medical, dental, and allied healthcare professional schools offer free clinics. My first experience in public interpreting was for a New Year celebration organized by a Chinese student club in college. The event planner invited professors and department heads who were English speakers. Hence, she needed the dinner banquet to be bilingual. Getting your feet wet requires you to think outside the box. Be creative, be proactive in your search, and be available. Opportunities to start interpreting for others are around you.

The second hurdle for entering this field is the medical knowledge you will need to acquire. Here are examples of ways you can expand your medical knowledge. For example, you might consider taking medical terminology or anatomy & physiology courses offered by the community college. At most community colleges, you can take these courses without being accepted into any program. Depending on your geographic area, your community college might offer interpretation classes. You can also get a list of training programs on the International Medical Interpreter Association (IMIA) website. I do not know which one to endorse or to recommend to you; all I can advise is for you to do your research to verify their claims.

The third hurdle for entering this field is to become certified in medical interpreting. There are many certification exams out there. Some are at the national level, and some are not. Taking the right test will save you time and money. Becoming a certified medical interpreter is a game-changer. It gives you the credentials that you need, it opens job opportunities, and it is a title that earns you more income. Not all certifications are created equal. For example, most internally issued certifications do not serve as a credential externally. For instance, I have a stack of certifications mailed to me from my first job. They were positive recognitions and appreciations from customers, but they did not open any doors later on when I was ready to make the next career move.

The U.S. Government does not regulate medical interpreter certification as it does for court interpreters. Therefore, it is easy to get lost in the world of accreditations. In a basic online search, you will probably see acronyms like NCIHC, NCCA, CHIA, CHI, CCHI, CMI, NBCMI, and IMIA. Cannot wrap your head around the different certifications? Luckily, you do not need to become an expert to know which test to take. The rule of thumb about the best certification test to consider is the one that employers list in the job description. Ultimately, that is your golden ticket. The two well-recognized certifications for medical interpreters are CCHI and NBCMI. CCHI stands for Certification Commission for Healthcare Interpreters. NBCMI stands for the National Board of Certification for Medical Interpreters. Both CCHI and NBCMI certifications are on the national level. Some states have interpreter certification; for example, in the state of Washington, there are interpreter certification tests offered by the Washington State Department of Social and Health Services. You can do this research for your state.

Once you know which certification test to take, it is time to register and pay for the exam. After your registration and payment, you will be provided online instructions on how to schedule for the exam and access to study materials. Your scope of preparation is what is in the study materials. Some certification tests contain a simultaneous interpretation component. You can picture simultaneous interpretation like an act of juggling. You render the first sentence you heard while your ears are listening to the next sentence to come. That process repeats and continues without taking a pause. You must not let any minor hiccups stop this flow, because when you get out of the rhythm, you are in trouble. Becoming certified consists of the investment of your time and money. It is a desirable credential for your career advancement.

The last hurdle in becoming a medical interpreter is knowing who the employers are. Many local agencies hire freelancers for assignments. Some corporations provide language services to clients nationwide. You will find hiring company names from online searches. I recommend you take the time to assess and compare your current qualifications with the job descriptions. From there, you will know what you need to focus on in your preparation.

You should memorize as many medical terms as you can. Baidu®, Google Translate®, and similar apps are all good resources to look up a word. Remember, "To err is human." Your longevity in this career depends on being good at catching errors and being quick to get clarification, as well as give corrections as needed. Even after fourteen years, I still take the time to clarify when I am not 100% sure of what I heard. A good interpreter is a humble interpreter, because a mistake is just one word away. A professional interpreter never stops learning.

CHAPTER 4

PRACTICE SCENARIOS

The followings are mock-up visits of conversation between a provider and a Limited English Proficiency (LEP) patient. The scenarios are entirely made up for you to get a feel for how the verbal test is. Have fun practicing.

CARDIOLOGY OUTPATIENT VISIT

Provider: What brought you here?

LEP: I have chest pain and shortness of breath.

Provider: Can you climb two flights of stairs without having shortness of breath?

LEP: No, I cannot climb stairs. I get out of breath, and my chest is tight.

Provider: What past medical history do you have?

LEP: I have high blood pressure, high cholesterol, and glaucoma.

Provider: You also have A-fib. Are you taking any blood thinners?

LEP: I take one 81mg aspirin daily.

Provider: Excellent. It helps to decrease your chance of a stroke. What other medication do you take on a regular basis?

LEP: Here is a list of medications I take every day.

Provider: I will order a stress test and an echocardiogram.

Someone from radiology will call you to schedule those tests. Do you need any refills?

LEP: No, thank you, doctor.

Provider: Your echocardiogram will show me if there is any sign of an enlarged aorta.

EMERGENCY ROOM VISIT

Provider: How did you fall?

LEP: I do not know. I was dizzy.

Provider: Did you lose consciousness? Are you in any pain?

LEP: I think I lost consciousness. My head hurts, and I have nausea.

Provider: The nurse will give you anti-nausea medication. And I will order a CAT scan of your head.

NURSING ASSESSMENT

Nurse: I have two medications for you. Let me first scan your wristband. One of the medications is for pain. The other one is a heparin injection to prevent blood clots. I will listen to your heart and your lungs. Take a deep breath. Now breathe normally. This is normal saline to flush the tubing. Later, someone will come to help you with taking a shower.

LEP: I do not want to take a shower. Can I have a wipe down instead?

PCP VISIT

Nurse: What is the purpose of today's visit?

LEP: I have a fever, sore throat, and running nose.

Nurse: When did the fever start?

LEP: Two days ago.

Nurse: Let me take your vitals. Your blood pressure is 130/85. Your temperature is 100.4. What is your pain level right now from a scale of 0 to 10?

LEP: My sore throat is a 3. But my chest hurts when I cough, and it is a 10.

Nurse: Are you coughing up anything? What color is it?

LEP: I am coughing up yellow phlegm.

Nurse: I will let the provider know.

SURGERY CONSENT

Provider: Please verify your name and date of birth.

LEP: My name is Jane Doe, and my date of birth is January 1, 1945.

Provider: In your own words, what are you here for today?

LEP: I am here for cataract surgery of my right eye.

Provider: Yes. This informed consent states that you are here for cataract surgery with an intraocular lens implant. Is that correct?

LEP: Yes, it is for my right eye.

Provider: Do you have any of the following: advance healthcare directive, healthcare proxy, living will, or medical power of attorney?

| LEP: | No, I do not have any. |
| Provider: | We will take good care of you. The anesthesiologist will come to speak to you next. |

WELL-CHILD CHECKUP VISIT

Provider:	Is the baby feeding well? Are you breastfeeding or bottle feeding?
Mom:	We are doing both. The baby feeds once every 2-3 hours.
Provider:	That is excellent. Where does the baby sleep?
Mom:	The baby sleeps in his crib.
Provider:	That is great. We recommend that babies sleep in their cribs. We will repeat blood work to check his jaundice level and see if bilirubin has gone down. It will be a heel poke.

CHAPTER 5

MEDICAL SPECIALTIES AND SETTINGS
醫學專科與類型

Ambulatory department	門診部
Ancillary services	輔助服務
Anesthesiology	麻醉科
Audiology	聽力科
Cardiology	心臟科
Dental	牙科
Dermatology	皮膚科
Emergency room	急診室
Endocrinology	內分泌科
ENT/otorhinolaryngology	耳鼻喉科
Family medicine	家庭醫學科
Gastroenterology	腸胃科
General surgery	普通外科
Genetics	遺傳學
Geriatrics	老人科
Gynecology and obstetrician	婦產科
Hematology/oncology	血液科/腫瘤科
Home healthcare services	居家醫療保健服務
Hospice	安寧療護

Intensive care unit	加護病房
Infectious disease	傳染科
Infertility	不孕科
Labor and delivery	分娩和產房
Maternity and newborn care	產婦和新生兒照顧
Maternal fetal medicine	母胎醫學
Mental health	心理健康
Nephrology	腎病科
Neurology	神經科
Nursing home	療養院
Nutrition	營養學
Occupational therapy	生活職能治療
Ophthalmology	眼科
Optometry	驗光科
Orthopedics	骨科
Otorhinolaryngology	耳鼻喉科
Outpatient surgery	外科門診手術
Palliative care	舒緩治療
Pathology	病理學
Pediatrics	兒科
Physical therapy	物理治療
Prenatal care	產前檢查
Primary care	初級保健
Psychiatry	精神病學
Psychology	心理學
Podiatry	腳科

Pulmonology	肺科
Radiology	放射科
Rehabilitation	康復科
Respiratory therapy	呼吸治療
Rheumatology	風濕科
Skilled nursing facility	專業護理機構
Speech therapy	語言治療
Surgery	外科
Urgent care	緊急護理
Urology	泌尿科

CHAPTER 6

MEDICAL PROVIDER TITLES
醫療保健提供者名稱

Attending physician	主治醫師
Board certified	醫師協會認證
Case manager	個案經理
Chaplain	醫牧
Chief attending	主治醫師主任
Chief resident doctor	住院醫師主任
Clerkship	見習
Discharge planning	出院準備服務
Fellow	臨床研究住院醫師
Home aid	看護, 護理, 護工
Home healthcare	家庭醫療保健
Home health services	居家護理服務
Intern	實習
Junior	資淺
Licensed resident	醫師資格執照
Medical assistant	醫療助理
Medical examiner	法醫
Midwife	助產士
Nurse	護士
Nurse anesthetist	麻醉科護士

Nurse practitioner   執業護士 ─

Primary care physician 初級保健醫師

Physician assistant   助理醫師

Resident doctor   住院醫師

Senior   資深

Social worker   社工

Triage nurse   分診護士

Visiting nurse service 家訪護士服務 ─

CHAPTER 7

WHAT SYMPTOMS DO YOU HAVE?
您有什麼症狀?

Belching	打嗝
Bloating	脹氣
Blurry vision	視力模糊
Bump	隆起一塊
Chest pain	胸痛
Chest tightness	胸悶
Chills	發冷
Colic	腸絞痛
Collapse	虛脫, 倒下
Confusion	意識混亂
Constipation	便秘
Convulsion	驚厥
Cough	咳嗽
Cramp	絞痛, 抽筋
Cystocele	膀胱突出症
Diarrhea	腹瀉
Difficulty with	有困難
sleeping	睡覺困難
speech	說話困難

swallowing	吞嚥困難
urination	排尿困難
Dizziness	頭暈
Drowsy	昏昏欲睡
Earache	耳朵痛
Edema	水腫
Erosion	糜爛
Fall	跌倒
Fatigue	疲勞
Fever	發燒
Flu-like	類似流感的
Flutter	撲動
Fracture	骨折
Frequent urination	尿頻
Fuzzy	模糊的
Hard of hearing	重聽
Headache	頭痛
Hearing loss	聽力喪失
Heart racing	心跳加快
Hives	蕁麻疹
Incontinence	大小便失禁
Itchy eyes	眼睛發癢
Jaundice	黃疸
Loss of	沒有了
appetite	沒有食欲
balance	沒有平衡感

energy	沒有精神
function	沒有功能
interest	沒有興趣
strength	沒有力氣
Lump	塊狀物
Mass	腫塊
Memory loss	喪失記憶力
Migraine	偏頭痛
Muffled hearing	聲音模糊不清
Nasal congestion	鼻塞
Nasal discharge	鼻涕
Nausea	噁心
Night sweats	盜汗
Numbness	麻木
Pain	疼痛
ache	痛
burning	灼熱性
crampy	痙攣性
diffuse	到處都痛
dull	隱隱的
mild, moderate, severe	輕微, 中度, 劇烈
sharp	尖銳
shooting	刺痛
sore, soreness	酸痛
tender	觸痛
throbbing	抽痛

tingling	刺痛
pressure-like	壓迫性
Palpitation	心悸
Phlegm	痰
Poor sleep	睡眠不良
Post-nasal drip	鼻涕倒流
Pulling on the ear	拉扯耳朵
Rash	皮疹
Rectocele	直腸前突
Rigid	僵硬
Ringing in the ear	耳鳴
Runny nose	流鼻涕
Seizures	癲癇發作
Sensation	感覺
Shortness of breath	氣短
Sore, bedsore	瘡，褥瘡
Sore throat	喉嚨痛
Spasm	痙攣
Spit up	溢奶
Sprained	扭傷
Sputum	痰
Stuffy nose	鼻塞
Swelling	腫脹
Trance	恍惚
Tremor	震顫
Unconscious	不省人事

Vertigo   眩暈 一

Vomiting   嘔吐

Watery eyes   愛流眼淚 一

Weakness   軟弱無力

Wheezing   氣喘 一

CHAPTER 8

WHAT MEDICATIONS DO YOU TAKE AT HOME?
您在家使用, 服用什麼藥物?

Albuterol	硫酸沙丁胺醇
Anthelmintic	抗蠕蟲藥物
Antibiotic	抗生素藥物
amoxicillin	阿莫西林
azithromycin	阿奇霉素
bleomycin	博來霉素
cefdinir	頭孢地尼
cephalosporins	頭孢菌素類
doxycycline	多西環素
erythromycin	紅霉素
penicillin	青霉素
sulfa group	磺胺類
tetracycline	四環黴素
vancomycin	萬古黴素
Anticoagulant	抗凝血劑
Antifungal	抗真菌藥物
Antihistamine	抗組胺藥物
Antiparasitic	抗寄生蟲藥物
Antiviral	抗病毒藥物

acyclovir	阿昔洛韋
lopinavir-ritonavir	抗HIV病毒藥物
remdesivir	抗埃博拉病毒藥物
ribavirin	病毒唑
tamiflu	特敏福
quinine	抗瘧疾藥物
Atorvastatin	阿托伐他汀
Beta receptor blocker	β受體阻滯劑
Blood thinner	血液稀釋劑
aspirin	阿斯匹林
coumadin	香豆素
heparin	肝素
warfarin	華法令
Codeine	可待因
Cortisol steroid	皮質類固醇
betamethasone	倍他米松
dexamethasone	地塞米松
hydrocortisone	氫化可的松
prednisone	強的松
Decongestant	通鼻藥，化痰藥
Diuretics	利尿劑
furosemide	速尿靈
hydrochlorothiazide	氫氯噻嗪
Gabapentin	加巴噴丁
Hormone	荷爾蒙
adrenalin	腎上腺素

aldosterone 醛固酮

estrogen 雌激素

progesterone 黃體酮

testosterone 睪酮

Hydrocodone 氫可酮

Ibuprofen 布絡芬

Inhaler 氣霧劑

metered dose inhalers 定量吸入器

spacer 儲霧罐

Insulin 胰島素

Lisinopril 賴諾普利

Medicated patch 藥物貼劑

Metformin 二甲雙胍

Metoprolol 美托洛爾

Nasal spray 鼻噴劑

Nitroglycerin sublingual 硝酸甘油舌下片

Omeprazole 奧美拉唑

Ranitidine 雷尼替丁

Sleep aid 助眠藥

Steroid 類固醇

Thrombolytic 溶栓藥

Thyroxine 甲狀腺素

Tylenol 太諾

Valsartan 纈沙坦

CHAPTER 9

HAVE YOU RECEIVED THE VACCINATIONS?
您接種過疫苗了嗎?

BCG	卡介苗
Diphtheria, tetanus, pertussis	百日咳、白喉、破傷風
Epidemic meningitis	流行性腦膜炎
Flu/Influenza	流感
Hemophilus influenzae type b	b型流感嗜血杆菌
Hepatitis A	甲肝
Hepatitis B	乙肝
HPV	人類乳突病毒
Japanese encephalitis	日本腦炎
Measles, mumps, rubella	麻疹, 腮腺炎, 風疹
Meningococcal	腦膜炎球菌
Pneumococcal	肺炎球菌
conjugate	兒童肺炎球菌结合疫苗
polysaccharide	肺炎球菌多糖疫苗
Polio	小兒麻痺症
Poliomyelitis	脊髓灰質炎
Rabies	狂犬病
Rotavirus	輪狀病毒
Shingles	帶狀皰疹

Smallpox	天花
Typhoid	傷寒
Varicella/chickenpox	水痘

CHAPTER 10

WHAT MEDICAL HISTORY DO YOU HAVE?
您的病史有哪些?

Anaphylaxis	過敏反應
Acid reflux	胃酸逆流
Addison disease	阿狄森氏病
Allergies	過敏
Alzheimer's disease	阿茲海默症
Anemia	貧血
Aneurysm	動脈瘤
Angioma	血管瘤
Apoptosis	細胞凋亡
Appendicitis	闌尾炎
Arthritis	關節炎
Aspirated pneumonia	吸入性肺炎
Asthma	哮喘病
Asthma attack	哮喘發作
Atherosclerosis	動脈粥狀硬化
Autism	自閉症
Bell's palsy	貝爾氏麻痺
Bleeding disorder	出血性疾病
Blepharoptosis	眼瞼下垂

Blood clot	血塊
Blood disorder	血液性疾病 一
Bone	骨頭
dislocation	錯位
fracture	骨折
spur	增生 一
Bronchitis	支氣管炎
Cancer	癌症
acute myeloid leukemia	急性髓性白血病 一
adenocarcinoma	腺癌 一
intraepithelial neoplasia	上皮內瘤病變 一
in situ	原位
invasive	浸潤性
leukemia	白血病
lymphoma	淋巴瘤
malignant	惡性的
melanoma	黑色素瘤 一
metastasize	轉移
non-Hodgkin lymphoma	非霍奇金淋巴瘤
non-small cell lung cancer	非小細胞肺癌
osseous sarcoma	骨肉瘤 一
squamous cell carcinoma	鱗狀細胞癌
Celiac disease	腹腔疾病 一
Cerebral vascular disease	腦血管病 一 CVD
Chest pain	胸痛
Cholangitis	膽管炎 一

Cholecystitis/gallbladder attack	膽囊炎/膽囊發作
Cholecystolithiasis	膽囊結石
Choledocholithiasis	膽總管結石
Cholelithiasis	膽結石
Cholestasis	膽汁淤積
Chronic fatigue	慢性疲勞
Circulatory disease	循環系統疾病
Cirrhosis	肝硬化
Cognitive impairment	認知障礙
Common cold	普通感冒
Concussion	腦震盪
Congestive heart failure	充血性心力衰竭
Coronary artery disease	冠心病
COPD	慢性阻塞性肺病
COVID-19	新冠肺炎
Crohn's disease	克隆氏症
Cushingoid syndrome	庫興氏症候群
Cyst	囊腫
Cystic fibrosis	囊性纖維化
Cystocele	膀胱脫垂
Dementia	失智症
Diabetes	糖尿病
Diverticulosis	憩室病
Down syndrome	唐氏綜合症
Duct ectasia	乳導管擴張症
Dysphagia	吞嚥困難

Dyspnea	呼吸困難
Edema	水腫
Emphysema	肺氣腫
Enlarged	肥大, 增大
adenoid	腺樣體增大
heart	心臟肥大
prostate	前列腺肥大
Epilepsy	癲癇
Eyes	眼睛
astigmatism	散光
blind	失明
cataract	白內障
conjunctivitis, pink eye	結膜炎
diabetic retinopathy	糖尿病視網膜病變
esotropia	內斜視
exotropia	外斜視
floater	飛蚊症
glaucoma	青光眼
macular degeneration	黃斑部病變
retinal detachment	視網膜剝離
retinopathy	視網膜病變
strabismus	斜視
stye	針眼
Fat necrosis	脂肪壞死
Fibro lipoma	纖維脂肪瘤
Fibrosis	纖維化

Flu	流行性感冒
Fracture	骨折
closed fracture	閉合性骨折
spinal compression	脊柱壓縮性骨折
Gallbladder dyskinesia	膽囊收縮功能不良
Gallstone	膽結石
cholesterol gallstone	膽固醇結石
pigment gallstones	色素性膽結石
Ganglion cyst	腱鞘囊腫
Gastroesophageal reflux	胃食道逆流
Globus	癔球症, 咽部異物感
Glucose intolerance	葡萄糖不耐症
Goiter	甲狀腺腫
Gout	痛風
Graft versus host disease	移植物對抗宿主疾病
Guillain-Barre syndrome	格林-巴利綜合症
Heart attack	心臟病發作
Heart disease	心臟病
Heart murmur	心臟雜音
Heart valve replacement	心臟瓣膜置換術
Hemangioma	血管瘤
Hemoptysis	咯血
Hemorrhage	出血
Hemorrhoid	痔瘡
Hepatitis A, B, C	甲肝, 乙肝, 丙肝
Hepatomegaly	肝腫大

Herniated disc	椎間盤突出
High blood pressure	高血壓
Huntington's disease	亨丁頓舞蹈症
Hydronephrosis	腎積水
Hyperactivities	好動
Hypertension	高血壓
Hyperthyroidism	甲狀腺機能亢進
Hypotension	低血壓
Hypothyroidism	甲狀腺功能減退
Infection	感染
bacterial	細菌性
c.diff	艱難梭菌　柯林
ebola	伊波拉病毒
E-Coli	大腸桿菌
Epstein-Barr virus	愛潑斯坦-巴爾病毒
fungal	真菌性
HIV	愛滋病病毒
HPV	人類乳頭瘤病毒
h-pylori	幽門螺旋桿菌
human herpesvirus 4	人類皰疹病毒第四型
mononucleosis	傳染性單核細胞增多症
MRSA	耐甲氧西林金黃色葡萄球菌
novel coronavirus	新型冠狀病毒
respiratory syncytial virus	呼吸道融合病毒
rotavirus	輪狀病毒
salmonella	沙門氏桿菌

SARS	非典型性肺炎
simple herpes	單純皰疹
staph: staphylococcus	葡萄球菌
strep throat	鏈球菌性咽喉炎
vancomycin-resistant enterococcus	萬古黴素抗藥性腸球菌
viral	病毒性
yeast	酵母菌
zika virus	茲卡病毒
Insomnia	失眠症
Intestinal metaplasia	(胃黏膜)腸上皮化生
Jaundice	黃疸
Kawasaki disease	川崎病
Kidney stone	腎結石
Laryngitis	喉炎
Leptomeningeal disease	軟腦膜病
Lesion	病變
Lupus	紅斑狼瘡
Lyme disease	萊姆病
Lymphangiectasia	淋巴管擴張
Lymphedema	淋巴水腫
Mastitis	乳腺炎
Mastoiditis	乳突炎
Meniere's disease	梅尼爾氏症
Meniscus injury	半月板損傷
Mental disorder	精神障礙

anorexia	厭食症
anxiety	焦慮症
attention deficit - hyperactivity disorder	注意力不足過動症
autism	自閉症
bipolar disorder	躁狂抑鬱症
catatonia	緊張性神經症
depression	抑鬱症
panic attack	驚恐發作
reactive mental disorder	反應性精神障礙
schizophrenia	精神分裂症
Multiple myeloma	多發性骨髓瘤
Muscular dystrophy	肌肉萎縮症
Myasthenia gravis	重症肌無力
Myelitis	脊髓炎
transverse	橫向的
Narcolepsy	嗜睡症
Nephrosis	腎病
Neuroblastoma	神經母細胞瘤
Neuropathy	神經病變
Neutropenic	中性粒細胞減少
Nodule	結節
Pancreatitis	胰腺炎
Paralysis	癱瘓
Parkinson's disease	帕金森病
Patent ductus arteriosus	動脈導管未閉

Peripheral neuritis	周邊神經病變
Perforation	穿孔
Phimosis	包莖
Plantar fasciitis	足底筋膜炎
Pleurisy	肋膜炎
Pneumoconiosis	肺塵病
asbestosis	石棉肺
black lung disease	黑肺症
Pneumonia	肺炎
Pneumothorax	氣胸
Polycystic kidney disease	多囊性腎病
Polyps	息肉
Post-polio syndrome	小兒麻痺後遺症
Pre-eclampsia	子癲前症
Prostate disease	前列腺疾病
Pulmonary embolism	肺栓塞
Respiratory distress	呼吸窘迫
Rheumatoid arthritis	類風濕性關節炎
Rhinitis	鼻炎
Sarcoidosis	結節病
Sarcoma	肉瘤
Scarlet fever	猩紅熱
Sciatica nerve pain	坐骨神經痛
Sclerosis	硬化
amyotrophic lateral sclerosis	肌萎縮性側索硬化症
multiple sclerosis	多發性硬化

Seizure	癲癇
Senility	衰老
Shingles	帶狀皰疹
Sickle cell anemia	鐮狀細胞性貧血
Skin	皮膚
acne, baby acne	痤瘡
cellulitis	蜂窩組織炎
cradle cap	乳痂
eczema	濕疹
psoriasis	銀屑病
rash	皮疹
scabies	疥瘡
seborrheic dermatitis	脂漏性皮膚炎
urticaria	蕁麻疹
Sleep apnea	睡眠呼吸暫停
Spondylolisthesis	脊椎滑脫
STD, sexual transmitted disease	性病
AIDS	愛滋病
AIDS related complex	愛滋病相關綜合症
chlamydia	衣原體
gonorrhea	淋病
herpes	皰疹
respiratory syncytial virus	呼吸道合胞病毒
syphilis	梅毒
trichomonas	牛滴蟲
venereal warts	性病疣

Steatorrhea	脂肪瀉
Stomach ulcer	胃潰瘍
Stroke	中風
Substances, controlled	管制藥物
barbiturate	巴比妥酸鹽
cocaine	可卡因
crack Cocaine	古柯鹼
ecstasy	狂喜
heroin	海洛英
LSD	迷幻藥
marijuana	大麻
methadone	美沙酮
methamphetamine	安非他命
opioid	鴉片
sedative	鎮靜劑
stimulant	興奮劑
Swelling	腫脹, 浮腫
Syringomyelia	脊髓空洞症
Thalassemia	地中海貧血症
Tic syndrome	抽動綜合症
Tick bites	蜱蟲叮咬
Tinnitus	耳鳴
Tonsillitis	扁桃腺炎
Tourette's syndrome	妥瑞症
Transient ischemic attack	短暫性腦缺血發作
Tuberculosis	結核病

active	開放性結核病
latent	潛伏結核感染
Tumor	腫瘤
benign breast tumor	良性乳腺腫瘤
pituitary tumor	垂體瘤
Ulceration	潰瘍
Urinary tract infection	尿道感染
Urticaria	蕁麻疹
Upper respiratory infection	上呼吸道感染
Vertigo	眩暈症
Whooping cough	百日咳

CHAPTER 11

WHAT IS MY BLOOD WORK RESULT?
我的血液檢查結果如何?

Albumin	白蛋白
Alkaline phosphatase	鹼性磷酸酶
Amylase	澱粉酶
Antibodies	抗體
Antigen	抗原
Bicarbonate	碳酸氫鹽
Bilirubin	膽紅素
Calcium	鈣
Carcinoembryonic antigen	癌胚抗原
Cholesterol	膽固醇
Complete blood count	全血細胞計數
Creatine kinase	肌酸激酶
Creatinine	肌酐
Ferrin	鐵蛋白
Globulin	球蛋白
Glucose	葡萄糖
HDL	高密度膽固醇
Hepatitis B e-antigen	乙肝e抗原
Hepatitis B surface antigen	乙肝表面抗原

Hepatitis core antibody	乙肝核心抗體
HIV test	愛滋病測試
Kidney function test	腎功能檢查
LDH	乳酸脫氫酶
LDL	低密度膽固醇
Liver function test	肝功能檢查
Lymphocytes	淋巴細胞
Magnesium	鎂
Phosphate	磷酸鹽 鎂
Plasma cell	漿細胞
Platelet	血小板
Potassium	鉀
Prostate specific antigen	前列腺特異抗原
Protein	蛋白質
Sodium	鈉
Thyroid stimulating hormone	促甲狀腺激素
Total lipid	總膽固醇
Triglyceride	三酸甘油酯
Troponin	肌鈣蛋白
Urea	尿素
Urea nitrogen	尿素氮
Uric acid	尿酸
Viral load	病毒量

CHAPTER 12

DOCTOR'S ORDERS
醫生開的檢查項目

Arterial blood gas	動脈血氣分析
Biopsy	切片檢查/活組織檢驗
Blood work	血液檢查
Chemo treatment	化療
Colonoscopy	大腸鏡檢查
EKG	心電圖
Electroconvulsive therapy	電驚厥療法
Electroencephalogram	腦電圖
Electromyography	肌電圖
HIDA scan	亞氨基二乙酸肝膽胰膽道攝影
Light therapy	照光治療
Lung function test	肺功能檢查
Mammogram	乳房攝影檢查
Mental state exam	精神狀態測試
MRI	磁共振造影
Newborn screening	初生兒篩檢
Nuchal translucency scan	頸部透明帶掃描
Nucleic acid test	核酸檢驗法
Pap smear	子宮頸抹片檢查
Pregnancy test	懷孕測試

Radiation treatment	放療
Rectal exam	肛門指檢
Stool sample test	糞便樣本檢查
Swab test	咽拭子採集
nasopharyngeal swab	鼻咽拭子
oropharyngeal swab	口咽拭子
TB skin test	結核菌皮膚測試
test negative	測試呈陰性
test positive	測試呈陽性
Ultrasound	超聲波
color doppler	彩色多普勒超聲波
echocardiogram	超聲心動圖
endoscopic ultrasound	內窺鏡超聲波
vaginal ultrasound	陰道超聲波, 陰超
Upper endoscopy	胃鏡檢查/上消化道內窺鏡
Urine test, urinalysis	尿檢
X-ray	X光片
chest	胸片,胸部X光片

CHAPTER 13

MEDICAL PROCEDURE/SURGERY
醫療程序/手術

-ectomy

cholecystectomy	膽囊切除術
colectomy	結腸切除術
gingivectomy	牙齦切除術
hysterectomy	子宮切除術
orchidectomy	睪丸切除術
salpingectomy	輸卵管切除術
thyroidectomy	甲狀腺切除術
transoral cholecystectomy	經口膽囊切除術

-gram

cholangiogram	膽管造影
intraoperative cholangiogram	術中膽管造影
radionuclide cystogram	放射性核素膀胱造影

-graphy

cholangiopancreatography	胰膽管造影

-haphy

colporrhaphy	陰道修補術
herniorrhaphy	疝氣修補術

-oscopy

bronchoscopy	支氣管鏡檢查

colonoscopy	結腸鏡檢查
laparoscopy	腹腔鏡檢查
laryngoscopy	喉鏡檢查術
upper endoscopy	上消化道胃鏡檢查

-ostomy

cecostomy	盲腸造口術
cholecystojejunostomy	膽囊空腸吻合術
ileostomy	迴腸造口術
nephrostomy	經皮腎造口術
salpingostomy	輸卵管造口術
tracheostomy	氣管切開術

-otomy

sphincterotomy	括約肌切開術

-plasty

blepharoplasty	眼瞼整形術
Aneurysm clip	動脈瘤夾
Biopsy	活組織檢查, 活檢
core needle biopsy	粗針穿刺活檢
excisional biopsy	切除式組織活檢
fine needle aspiration	細針穿刺抽吸活檢
MRI guided biopsy	磁共振引導下的活檢
stereotactic biopsy	立體定向活檢
vacuum assisted biopsy	真空輔助活檢術
Central vein access catheter	中央靜脈導管
Circumcision	包皮環切術/割包皮
Common bile duct exploration	膽總管探查術

Dialysis	透析, 洗腎
peritoneal dialysis	腹膜透析
ECMO	葉克膜氧合器
Endoscopic biliary stenting	內窺鏡膽道支架置入術
Endoscopic surgery	內窺鏡手術
Endoscopic ultrasound	內視鏡超聲波
Endovascular coil	血管內線圈
Gastroduodenal anastomosis	胃十二指腸吻合術
Implanted drug pumps	植入式藥物泵
Intubation	插管
IV access port	靜脈注射座
Lumbar puncture	腰椎穿刺
Mechanical ventilation	人工呼吸機
Nerve block	神經阻滯
Non-invasive	無創, 非侵入性
PICC Line	週邊置入中心靜脈導管
Pins, plates, screws, wire	銷, 骨板, 骨螺絲, 鋼線
Portal vein catheter insertion	腔靜脈導管置入術
Post-surgical hardware	術後金屬
Programmable shunt	可調式分流器
Radiation seeds	放射性粒子
Radionuclide bone scan	放射性核素骨掃描
Shock-wave lithotripsy	震波碎石術
Spinal cage	脊椎間體護架
Spinal decompression, stabilize	脊椎減壓固定術
Spinal tap	腰椎穿刺

Tendon transfer	肌腱轉移術
Tissue expander	組織擴張器
Total knee replacement	全膝關節置換術
Ventriculoperitoneal shunt	腦室腹腔分流術

CHAPTER 14

CARDIOLOGY/CARDIOVASCULAR
心臟科/心血管科

List of irregular heart rhythm	不規則的心律
Atrial fibrillation	心房纖維顫動 (房顫)
Atrial flutter	心房撲動 (房撲)
Atrial premature beat	房性早搏
Premature ventricular contractions	室性早搏
Premature contraction	早搏
Ventricular arrhythmia	室性心律不正
Ventricular fibrillation	心室纖維性顫動
Ventricular flutter	心室撲動

Diagnosis	診斷
Aneurysm	動脈瘤
Angina	心絞痛
Aortic insufficiency	主動脈瓣閉鎖不全
Arrhythmia	心律不整
Arteritis	動脈炎
Atherosclerosis	動脈粥狀硬化
Atrial septal defect	心房中膈缺損
Bradycardia	心跳過慢
Bilateral pleural effusion	兩側肋膜積水

Blood clot	血塊
Cardiac arrest	心臟停搏
Cardiomegaly	心臟肥大
Cardiomyopathy	心肌病
Cerebrovascular accident	腦血管意外
Cerebrovascular disease	腦血管疾病
Chest compression	壓胸心肺復甦術
Congenital heart disease	先天性心臟病
Congestive heart failure	心臟衰竭
Coronary artery disease	冠狀動脈病
Deep vein thrombosis	深部靜脈栓塞
Dilated cardiomyopathy	擴張性心肌病
Dyspnea	呼吸困難
Embolism	栓塞
Endocarditis	心內膜炎
Enlarged heart	心臟肥大
Heart attack	心臟病發作
Heart failure	心臟衰竭
Heart murmur	心跳有雜音
Heart valve replacement	心臟瓣膜置換手術
Hypertension	高血壓
Hypotension	低血壓
Mitral insufficiency	二尖瓣閉鎖不全
Mitral regurgitation	二尖瓣返流
Mitral stenosis	二尖瓣狹窄
Mitral valve prolapse	二尖瓣脫垂

Myocardial infarction	心肌梗塞
Myocarditis	心肌炎
Patent ductus arteriosus	動脈導管未閉
Pericarditis	心包炎
Plaque	斑塊
Pulmonary embolism	肺栓塞
Pulmonary valve regurgitation	肺動脈瓣膜返流
Rheumatic heart disease	風濕性心臟病
Shock	休克
Stroke	中風
Tachycardia	心跳過快
Transient ischemic attack	短暫性缺血發作
Tricuspid valve prolapse	三尖瓣脫垂
Varicose veins	靜脈曲張

Testing	**檢查項目**
Angiogram	血管造影
Echocardiogram	超聲心動圖
EKG	心電圖
Holter monitoring	連續心電圖描記器
Radionuclide imaging	放射性核素成像
Stress test	心臟耐力負荷測試
exercise stress test	運動耐力測試
nuclear stress test	核心臟耐力負荷測試

Medical procedure	醫療程序
Angiogram	血管造影術
Angioplasty	氣球血管成形術
Artificial valve replacement	人工瓣膜置換
Atrial fibrillation ablation	心房顫動消融術
Cardiac ablation	心臟消融術
Cardiac catheterization	心導管術
Cardioversion	心臟電擊術
Coronary artery bypass surgery	冠狀動脈繞道手術
Defibrillator	除顫器
Inferior vena cava filter	下腔靜脈濾器置入術
Myocardial bridge	冠狀動脈心肌橋
Nuclear perfusion imaging	核心肌灌注掃描
Pacemaker	心臟起搏器
Resuscitation	心肺復甦術
Stent	支架

CHAPTER 15

ENT/OTORHINOLARYNGOLOGY
耳鼻喉科

Diagnosis	診斷
Acoustic neuroma	聽神經瘤
Deaf	聾子
Ear barotrauma	耳氣壓傷
Ear wax	耳垢
Hearing impaired	聽力受損
Hearing loss	聽力損失
conductive	傳導性聽力損失
sensorineural	感音神經性耳聾
Labyrinthitis	迷路炎
Mastoiditis	乳突炎
Meniere's disease	梅尼爾氏症
Otitis media with effusion	滲出性中耳炎
Perforated eardrum	鼓膜穿孔
Ruptured eardrum	鼓膜破裂
Swimmer's ear	游泳性耳炎
Tinnitus	耳鳴
Vertigo	眩暈
Vestibular disorder	前庭障礙

Test, Medical Procedure	檢驗、醫療程序
Audiometer	聽力計
Cochlear implant	人工耳蝸
Hearing test	聽力測試
Myringotomy	鼓膜切開術
Otologic surgery	耳外科
Otosclerosis	耳硬化症
Otoscope	耳鏡

CHAPTER 16

GYNECOLOGIST AND OBSTETRICIAN (OBGYN)
婦產科

Symptoms	症狀
Contraction	宮縮
Braxton-Hicks contraction	假性宮縮
Cramp	絞痛
Foul odor	惡臭，異味
Heavy period	月經過多
Irregular period	經期不規律
Itching	癢
Labor pain	分娩陣痛
Vaginal discharge	陰道分泌
Water break	破羊水

Diagnosis	診斷
Abruptio placenta	胎盤早期剝離
Adenomyosis	子宮腺肌病
Benign breast tumor	良性乳腺腫瘤
Breast cancer	乳腺癌
Cervical carcinoma	宮頸癌
Cervical dysplasia	宮頸非典型增生

Cervical erosion		宮頸糜爛
Cervical intraepithelial neoplasia		宮頸上皮內瘤樣病變 一
Cervicitis	CIN	宮頸炎
Cord blood		臍帶血 一
Cyst		囊腫
Cystocele		膀胱突出症
Ductal carcinoma in situ		乳管原位癌 一
Dysmenorrhea		經痛 一
Ectopic pregnancy		子宮外孕
Embryo sac		胚囊
Endometrial cancer		子宮內膜癌
Endometrial hyperplasia		子宮內膜增生
Endometrioid cystadenoma		子宮內膜囊腺瘤 一
Endometrioma		子宮內膜瘤
Endometriosis		子宮內膜異位症
Fibroadenoma		纖維腺瘤
Fibroid		子宮肌瘤
Fibro lipoma		纖維脂肪瘤 一
Full term		足月 一
Gestational diabetes		妊娠糖尿病
Group B strep infection		B組鏈球菌感染
Hemorrhage		出血
Infertility		不孕症
Mastitis		乳腺炎
Miscarriage		流產
Ovarian cyst		卵巢囊腫

Papillary tumor	乳頭狀瘤
Placenta previa	前置胎盤
Polyp	息肉
Postpartum depression	產後憂鬱症
Pre-eclampsia	妊娠毒血症
Preterm vs. full-term labor	早產和足月生產
Spinal bifida	脊柱裂
Squamous intraepithelial lesion	鱗狀上皮內病變
Stillborn	死胎
Tear	撕裂
Uterine fibroids	子宮纖維肌瘤
Uterine prolapse	子宮脫垂
Vaginitis	陰道炎
Yeast infection	酵母菌感染

Testing	**檢查項目**
Biopsy	活檢
cone	錐形活檢
needle	針刺活檢
Colposcopy	陰道鏡檢查
Glucose tolerance test	葡萄糖耐量測試
Hysteroscopy	宮腔鏡檢查
Pap smear	宮頸抹片檢查
Pelvic exam	下盆腔檢查
Pregnancy test	懷孕測試
Vaginal exam	陰道檢查

Medical Procedure	醫療程序
Ablation	消融術
Abortion	墮胎
medicated	藥物流產
induced	人工流產
spontaneous	自發流產
surgical	手術流產
threatened	先兆性流產
Amniocentesis	羊水穿刺 —
Augmented labor	催產 —
Caesarean delivery	剖腹產 —
Cervical cerclage	宮頸環紮術 —
Colporrhaphy	陰道修補術
Conization of the cervix	宮頸錐切術 —
Contraception	避孕
Cryotherapy	冷凍治療
D&C	刮宮
Embryo	胚胎
Epidural	無痛分娩 —
Episiotomy	會陰切開術 —
Hysterectomy	子宮切除術
Hysteroscopic	宮腔镜
Induced labor	引產
Intrauterine device	宮內節育器 IUD
Intrauterine spiral	子宮環 —
In vitro fertilization	試管嬰兒 —

LEEP procedure	宮頸環形電切術
Myomectomy	子宮肌瘤切除術
NuvaRing	避孕環
Sterilization	絕育
Tubal ligation, sterilization	輸卵管結紮術
Uterine fibroid embolization	子宮纖維肌瘤栓塞術

Medication	**藥物**
Birth control pills	避孕藥
Estrogen	雌激素
Folic acid	葉酸
Hormone therapy	荷爾蒙療法
Oxytocin	縮宮素
Pitocin	催產素
Prenatal vitamins	孕婦維生素
Progesterone	黃體酮

CHAPTER 17

DURABLE MEDICAL DEVICE
耐用的醫療設備

Bedpan	便盆
Boots	助行靴
Cane	拐杖
Cast	固定套
Chest tube	胸腔引流管
Commode, bedside toilet	馬桶椅
Crutches	腋下拐杖
Denture, false teeth	假牙
Feeding tube, NG tube	胃管, 鼻胃管
Foley catheter	導尿管
Hearing aid	助聽器
Behind the ear	耳後助聽器
Completely in the ear	全耳塞式助聽器
Open-fit	開放式助聽器
Ostomy pouch	造口袋
Oxygen	氧氣
CPAP machine	正壓呼吸機
Nasal cannula	鼻氧管
Nebulizer	霧化器
Oxygen face mask	氧氣面罩

Plaster cast	打石膏
Pulse oximeter	脈搏血氧計
Shower chair	淋浴椅
Sling	吊帶
Spirometer	肺活量計
Splint	固定夾板
Urinal	尿壺
Walker	助行器

CHAPTER 18

CENTERS FOR MEDICARE & MEDICAID SERVICES
醫療保險和醫療補助中心

The cms.gov is the website for Centers for Medicare & Medicaid Services. You can find helpful resources and forms in many languages. The CMMS related glossary can also be found on www.medicare.gov/publications.

Advance healthcare directive	醫療照護事前指示
Brand-name drugs	專利藥物
Catastrophic coverage	災難型保險計劃
Cost-sharing	分攤費用.
Co-insurance	共保額
Consolidated premium	綜合保險費
Copay	定額手續費
Coverage	承保範圍
Coverage gap	承保缺口
Deductible	自付款
Extra help	額外補助
FICA	聯邦保險稅法
First tier	第一等级
Hardship exemption	困難豁免的人們
Health care proxy	醫療代理

HMO	管理照顧計劃
Living will	生前意願書
Marketplace	健保市場
Medicaid	州醫療補助
Medical power of attorney	醫療授權委託書
Medicare	聯邦醫保
Medicare saving program	聯邦醫保省錢計劃
Medication therapy management	藥物治療管理計劃
Medigap	補充保險
Open enrollment	開放註冊期
Part A	A 部分 - 住院保險
Part B	B 部分 - 門診保險
Part C	C 部分 - 聯邦保險優勢計劃
Part D	D 部分 - 處方藥保險
Pay	支付
Plan	保險計劃
bronze, silver	青銅, 白銀
gold, platinum	黃金, 白金
PPO	首選醫療機構的保險計劃
Preferred generic drug	首選非專利藥
Self-employed	自業
Social security	社會安全福利
Social security statement	社會安全收入報表
Special enrollment	特別註冊期
SSI	社會安全生活補助金
Tiers of coverages	保險級別

HUMAN ANATOMY

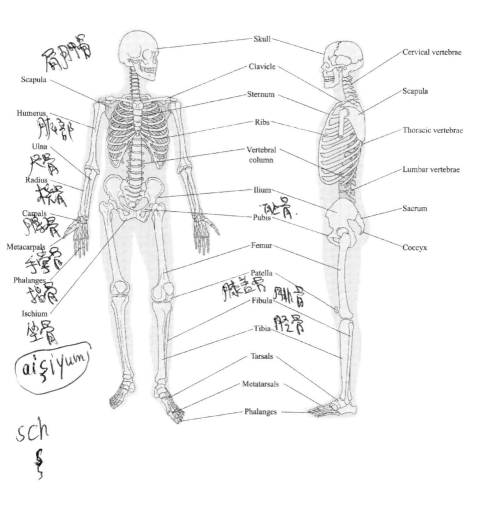

Skull
Clavicle
Sternum
Ribs
Vertebral column
Ilium
Pubis
Femur
Patella
Fibula
Tibia
Tarsals
Metatarsals
Phalanges

Cervical vertebrae
Scapula
Thoracic vertebrae
Lumbar vertebrae
Sacrum
Coccyx

Scapula
Humerus
Ulna
Radius
Carpals
Metacarpals
Phalanges
Ischium

HUMAN BRAIN

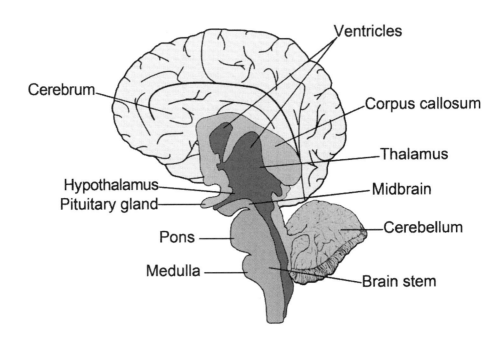

HUMAN EYE DIAGRAM

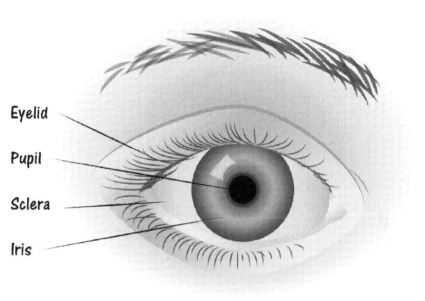

Eyelid
Pupil
Sclera
Iris

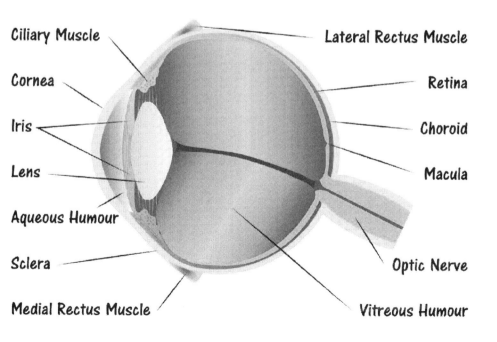

Ciliary Muscle
Cornea
Iris
Lens
Aqueous Humour
Sclera
Medial Rectus Muscle

Lateral Rectus Muscle
Retina
Choroid
Macula
Optic Nerve
Vitreous Humour

ANATOMY OF HUMAN EAR

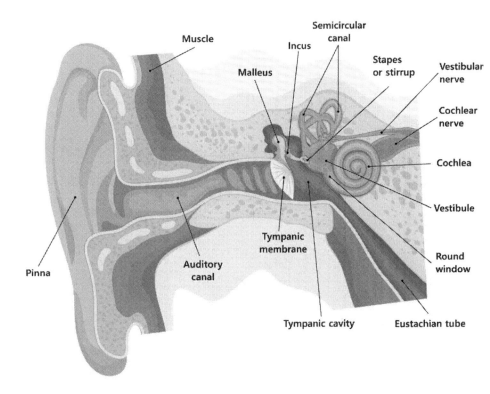

INTERNAL ANATOMY OF HEART

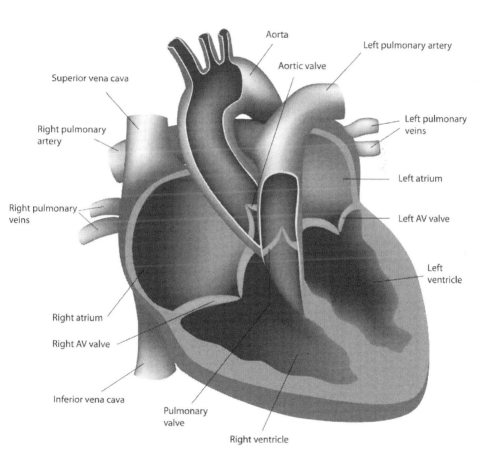

Aorta

Left pulmonary artery

Aortic valve

Superior vena cava

Right pulmonary artery

Left pulmonary veins

Right pulmonary veins

Left atrium

Left AV valve

Left ventricle

Right atrium

Right AV valve

Inferior vena cava

Pulmonary valve

Right ventricle

THE RESPIRATORY SYSTEM

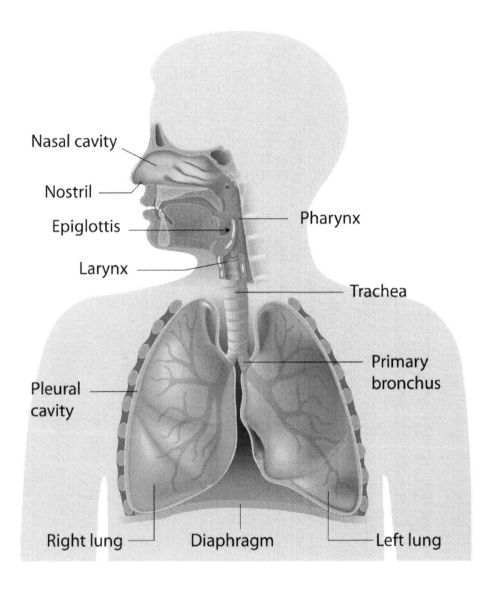

Nasal cavity

Nostril

Epiglottis

Pharynx

Larynx

Trachea

Primary bronchus

Pleural cavity

Right lung

Diaphragm

Left lung

ANATOMY OF INTESTINE

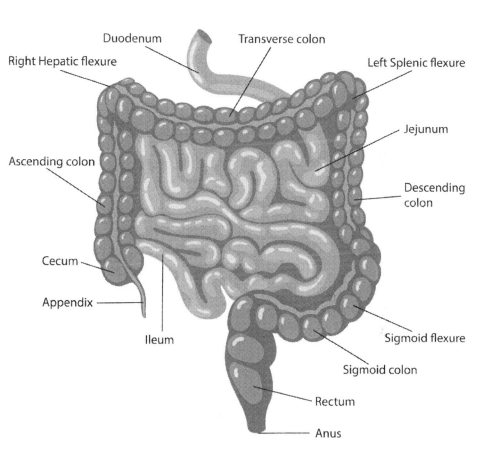

GALLBLADDER AND EXTRAHEPATIC BILE DUCT

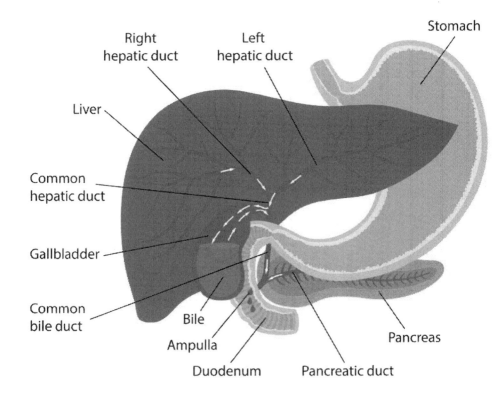

Stomach

Right hepatic duct

Left hepatic duct

Liver

Common hepatic duct

Gallbladder

Common bile duct

Bile

Ampulla

Duodenum

Pancreatic duct

Pancreas

HUMAN REPRODUCTIVE SYSTEM

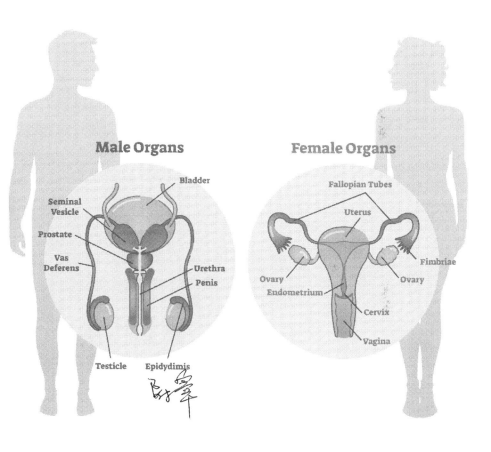

Male Organs

Bladder
Seminal Vesicle
Prostate
Vas Deferens
Urethra
Penis
Testicle
Epidydimis

Female Organs

Fallopian Tubes
Uterus
Fimbriae
Ovary
Ovary
Endometrium
Cervix
Vagina

Made in United States
Orlando, FL
14 January 2022